WHAT'S THE USE OF TRUTH?

What's the Use of

TRUTH?

Richard Rorty & Pascal Engel

Edited by Patrick Savidan
Translated by William McCuaig

 COLUMBIA UNIVERSITY PRESS   NEW YORK

Columbia University Press
Publishers Since 1893
New York, Chichester, West Sussex
A quoi bon la verité? © 2005 Editions Grasset et Fasquelle
Copyright © 2007 Columbia University Press
All rights reserved

Library of Congress Cataloging-in-Publication Data

Rorty, Richard
(A quoi bon la verité. English)
What's the use of truth? / Richard Rorty and Pascal Engel /
edited by Patrick Savidan ; translated by William McCuaig.
p. cm.
Includes bibliographical references.
ISBN-10: 0-231-14014-2 (alk. paper)
ISBN-13: 978-0-231-14014-0
1. Truth. I. Engel, Pascal, 1954– II. Savidan, Patrick, 1965–
III. Title.

BD171.E5313   2007
121—dc22   2006029199

c 10 9 8 7 6 5 4 3

Contents

Patrick Savidan

The public debate from which this book results was held at the Sorbonne in November 2002, organized by the Collège de philosophie. It could not have been more lively. What provided the spark was the extent of the divergence between the points of view of our two guests, especially with regard to their conceptions of truth as well as their ideas of what we should expect from it.

One is indeed tempted to review the respective trajectories of Richard Rorty and Pascal Engel with the idea of fundamental divergence in mind, for the reader will find the subject of truth illuminated vividly from two very different angles in this debate. The American philosopher Richard Rorty

was trained in the discipline of analytic philosophy and pragmatism, but he soon began to defend the work of authors like Heidegger, Foucault,
and Derrida. In contrast, Pascal Engel received his
early philosophical formation within a system that
was, to say the least, unreceptive to the virtues of
analytic philosophy, and yet, as a philosopher, he
has engaged exclusively in high-level work on the
themes and the works, and made use of the meth-
ods, of analytic philosophy.

The interest of this debate obviously exceeds
this topologico-intellectual background. It arises
mainly from the point at issue: what is truth?
What value should we see in it or attribute to it?

Starting from the pragmatist premises that he
has made his own, Richard Rorty conducts a de-
termined campaign against realism, relying especially on the work of Arthur Fine, the philosopher
of science, and on that of Donald Davidson and
Robert Brandom. His thesis is, roughly speaking,
the following: the realism-antirealism debate is
passé because we are progressing toward a conception of thought and language that accepts that
these may be considered as not containing representations of reality. As realism subsides, it will be

possible to escape from the Cartesian problematic of the subject and the object and to break free of the ancient one of appearance and reality. As Rorty writes in "A Pragmatist View of Contemporary Analytic Philosophy," "We shall no longer be tempted to practice either epistemology or ontology."[1] This radical thesis does not affect philosophical specialisms alone; it also induces a profound transformation of philosophical practice.

We must ponder carefully what is at stake in this challenge to the philosophy of representation, philosophy as the "mirror of nature," as Richard Rorty puts it in the title of his celebrated book.[2] For him, the attitude of those who remain in thrall to the demands of a naive natural ontology— those who feel a sort of devotion to realism—is analogous to that of the religious believer. As he has written in this connection, "Reality as it is in itself, apart from human needs and interests is, in my view, just another of the obsequious Names of God"; this "heartfelt devotion to realism" is "the Enlightenment's version of the religious urge to bow down before a non-human power."[3] In this sense, then, the pragmatism of Richard Rorty lies in combating the residues of servility still left in place by the Enlightenment. It is necessary, in his view, to go beyond the critique of superstition and subject the realist presuppositions and pretensions of modern representationist philosophy to critique as well. Hence he proposes to renounce the notions of "philosophical method" and "philosophical problems," which for him are no more than the "unfortunate consequence of the over-professionalization of philosophy which has disfigured this area of culture since the time of Kant."[4]

The question is of course to determine to what extent this charge is legitimate. Might it only be "true"? Let us turn to our two philosophers. Pascal Engel speaks first.

Translator's Note

The translation was made in collaboration with the editor and both authors. Pascal Engel and Richard Rorty have each checked and made revisions to their portions of the text for this English version of their debate.

WHAT'S THE USE OF TRUTH?

As Bernard Williams remarks at the start of his recent book, *Truth and Truthfulness*, two currents that
appear to clash with one another coexist in contemporary society.[1] On one hand, there has never
been so much distrust of the values of rationality,
scientific progress, truth, and objectivity, either in
advanced intellectual circles or in the media and
society generally. On the other, never has the impression that we are being deceived by the authorities (political and scientific) that are supposed
to guarantee precisely these values, and the need
for trust, been so great.[2] Why, if we no longer believe in truth, is there such a longing for it? Is it
one of those familiar paradoxes, by which, having

1

abandoned religion, we continue to search for a substitute or by which, when we no longer accept authority, we still shrink from getting rid of it entirely? It always used to astonish me, when I was attending Michel Foucault's courses at the Collège de France in the 1970s, to hear him explaining to us that the notion of truth was no more than an instrument of power, and that, since all power was bad, truth could only be the expression of some malign intent, and then see him marching in demonstrations under banners bearing the slogan Truth and Justice. Why do journalists, who claim that their professional code of ethics and their duty not to spread untruths are important to them, so often show indulgence toward thinkers who tell them that truth and rationality are empty words? And yet—are these necessarily examples of incoherence and cynicism? Perhaps people mistrust truth as an abstract ideal, in the name of which many authorities claim to exert their sway, but aspire to it in their daily lives. Maybe they don't believe in truth as an intrinsic value, an ultimate goal, while still believing in truth as an instrumental value serving other purposes, like happiness or freedom. We dislike preachers who speak in the name of Truth, but we pay attention to everyday truths, like the ones in the periodic statement of our bank balance. But, then, what is the concept of truth we are meant to reject, and what is the one we are meant to cling to? Should we reject both? Or should we hold on to both? Is it really coherent to say that one doesn't want Truth but is ready to accept that there are theories, statements, or beliefs, that are true?

There is a wrong way to put these questions, which is simply to set the postmodernists, the relativists, and all who believe that truth is an empty word—we could call them veriphobes[3]—on one side and the defenders of the ideals at which the veriphobes scoff on the other. The result is predictable: not only does each side dig in its heels, they wind up resembling each other. Those who attack truth and reason as oppressive values (as male values, for example, in some feminist polemics) end up being just as puritan as those whom they oppose. In fact, it is not the rationalists who provoke a reign of terror and censorship. It is those who cultivate a systematic suspicion about words like *truth, reason,* or *objectivity* ("cachez ces guillemets que je ne saurais voir"). The same opponents of rationalism pose as victims unjustly attacked by a dogmatic and reactionary establishment. The Sokal hoax furnished us with examples of a conflict of this type,[4] always on the verge of degenerating into rhetoric on both sides. Contemporary anti-rationalism and its political correctness have had such success in dramatizing these oppositions that whoever ventures to recall the existence of certain cognitive values when faced with palpable viola-tions of them is immediately accused of being a puritanical censor or a moralizer.[5]

Richard Rorty has often been seen, by post-modernism's crustier adversaries, as the villain of the piece, all the more so in that he has ex-pressed—with the clarity and simplicity that char-acterize his prose—ideas that authors like Fou-cault, Deleuze, Derrida, and Latour (to cite only French examples) have expressed in a more florid or abstruse style and has explicitly defended their works and their thematic ideas in the face of the hostility of analytical philosophers. At a certain point he started to look like the official philoso-pher of veriphobia, becoming the philosophical illustration of Alfred Hitchcock's maxim "the better the villain, the better the movie." But to see Rorty simply as a staunchly relativistic post-modernist would be to misunderstand totally his work and the interest of his analyses. His position in these debates is entirely individual and original. For one thing, even though it is a long time since he claimed to be an analytic philosopher, he was one at the outset of his career and still debates on an equal footing with philosophers in this tradition, argument for argument. Unlike authors such as Derrida, who give the impression that analytic philosophy is perfectly alien to them, Rorty knows exactly what he is talking about when he discusses the theses of analytic philosophers.[6] For another thing, Rorty sees himself as the scion of American pragmatism, and his analyses of the notion of truth belong in the lineage of James and Dewey in particular. Many of his arguments are derived from Quine, Davidson, and Sellars (even though he interprets them in his own way).[7] Unlike the relativistic postmodernists, he has put forward arguments aiming to show that truth does not have the importance usually attributed to it. These arguments are very much worthy of study. But let me try to state why they do not convince me.

Richard Rorty claims a place in the American pragmatist tradition. But his pragmatism is very different from that of the founder of this current, C.S. Peirce.[8] I hope that the following is not an unfair sketch of Rorty's positions on truth.[9]

1. The notion of truth has no explanatory use and does not cover any essence or substance or designate any profound substantial or metaphysical property or any object (the True).

2. In particular, the traditional realist notion of truth as the correspondence between our statements, judgments, or propositions and reality, or "the facts," and, in general, any theory of thought as representation of reality are devoid of meaning.

3. In consequence, the debates between realism and antirealism, which still unsettle much of contemporary analytic philosophy, are hollow.

4. The problem is not to make our statements true but to justify them, and there is no distinction to be made between truth and justification. Justification itself is nothing other than agreement among the members of a group or a community, and there is no ultimate, final agreement or ideal convergence of statements.

5. The concept of truth being empty, truth cannot be a norm of scientific or philosophical inquiry or an ultimate goal of our search. A fortiori, neither can it be a value.

6. From the fact of having rejected these mythical notions of truth, it does not follow that there is nothing to say about the world: there are causal, natural relations between the world and ourselves which we can study. But, all the same, it would be vain to hope to obtain a naturalistic, reductionist theory of representation and intentionality.

7. The fact that objectivity and truth do not matter does not signify that there are not certain values to defend; the values in question are those habitually promoted by the pragmatist tradition—those of solidarity, tolerance, liberty, and the sense of community. These values make it a great deal more feasible to promote democracy than the Kantian and utilitarian reconstructions of justice that have dominated the moral and political philosophy of the last thirty years. Rorty is too well aware of the difficulties of James's pragmatism in this area to claim to *assimilate* truth to utility: that which is useful may be false and that which is false may be useful.[10] But this does not shake his

conviction that the values of social utility should predominate over the values of truth.

In arguing for these positions, Rorty relies to a large extent on what is called a deflationist or minimalist theory of truth. There are many versions of this view, and it is not possible to discuss all of them here.[11] Rorty's version consists in the claim that there is nothing more to truth (nothing more fundamental, explanatory, or "metaphysical") than the following ways of using the word *true*:

1. an *endorsing* or *performative* use: *true* serves to express endorsement of a statement;
2. a cautionary use, as when one says, "your belief that P is justified, but it is not true";
3. a disquotational use, resting on the equivalence that warrants the move from asserting "P" to asserting " 'P' is true'" as well as the reverse.

According to Rorty, there are no other uses, and no other hidden meanings, of the word *true*. When we say that P is true, all we are doing, he tells us, is concurring with P, "giving it a little rhetorical pat on the back" or a "compliment." When we say that P is perhaps justified, but not true, our caution simply expresses the fact that P cannot be adopted as a rule of action, and that we might encounter an audience who would refuse P. (Thus the cautionary use does not in the least acknowledge that *reality* might disprove the justification for our belief.) As the fourth of the positions outlined above states, there is no difference for Rorty between truth and justification, and no difference between objective justification and justification for a given community (this is what might be called, following Williams, the thesis of the *indistinguishability* of truth and justification).[12] Truth is neither rational acceptability at the limit of inquiry, as C.S. Peirce, Hilary Putnam, and Crispin Wright all maintain to varying degrees, nor the ideal convergence within a communicational community, as in Habermas. Finally, the disquotational use signals that true is simply a device we use to speak about statements and approve them, not a term designating an objective world that transcends the approval we express to our audience and our own community. Given that the concept of truth is so slender and insubstantial, it follows that the epistemic role normally assigned to truth—to be the norm or goal of our inquiries, especially scientific inquiry—is quite simply impossible to fulfill. Truth is neither a norm nor an ultimate goal.[13] It cannot be a norm in the sense of that which regulates inquiry because it is unknowable. And it cannot be an ultimate goal in the sense of being an intrinsic value (although it can have an instrumental value). Thus there is no point in invoking it, either in science, in philosophy, in ethics, or in politics.

These positions have a certain skeptical and nihilistic ring; often they are characterized as relativist. But Rorty denies being a relativist with respect to truth, for when the relativist says "There is no truth other than what is true for me," he is using the word true in a *descriptive* sense. Now Rorty maintains that this word has no descriptive meaning, only an expressive one: it communicates a state of the speaker and her approval to her audience.[14] Still, I do not believe that Rorty is an eliminativist with respect to truth, like certain deflationists who defend a "redundancy" theory of truth: since there is nothing more to P than "it is true that P," there is no need to retain the predicate true, which becomes superfluous.[15] Rorty in contrast does not propose to jettison this word altogether and banish it from our vocabulary. What he does do is to try to scrub away the illusions and myths that cling to it. This is why he generally prefers to be called an ironist or a quietist.

My reaction to Rorty's theses is much like that of some of his critics, who are attracted to the themes he develops, but who find that he carries them to extremes. Let me begin by stating the points on which I agree with him.

I agree with Rorty that the word true has a minimal meaning, which is roughly given by the disquotational schema illustrated in Tarski's celebrated equivalence—"Snow is white" is true if and only if snow is white. The whole question turns on whether the meaning of *true* boils down to this disquotational use. I likewise agree on the fact that the classical theory of truth as correspondence runs up against considerable difficulties and that none of the contemporary conceptions that attempt to revive it (like those of the Australian metaphysicians) is satisfactory.[16] I also have a good deal of sympathy for certain pragmatist themes put forward by Rorty and by the tradition to which he belongs, and I have even defended certain pragmatist positions myself, notably those of authors like Peirce and Ramsey.[17] I also think that his attempts to demythologize the notion of truth are salutary and useful. When we reflect that truth is the favorite word of religious sects and fundamentalists of every kind, we can only concur with Rorty on the need to be wary of it.

But, for all that, the area of my agreement with Rorty is still rather small. I do not believe that, because the correspondence theory of truth encounters difficulties that are perhaps insurmountable, it follows that we must surrender any realist conception of truth, nor, contrary to thesis 2 above, that we can totally rid philosophy of oppositions between realism and antirealism in every field. I also think that truth is a norm of inquiry.[18] The sense in which it is a norm has to be spelled out carefully, but this is not the place to argue these points. The fact is that, although he is anything but a philosopher who refuses debate, Richard Rorty has often defended a highly therapeutic vision of philosophy, quite close to the one often attributed to Wittgenstein. He maintains that interesting philosophy is rarely the analysis of the pros and cons of a thesis, but rather that it consists in an attempt to replace one vocabulary with another and bring it about that philosophers and all those who speak as they do should gradually cease to express themselves in a certain way. Thus—for him—we ought to stop speaking of truth as the representation of the real, as an ultimate goal, and so on, and try to *redescribe* what we usually describe using this vocabulary by means of a different one stripped clean of these mythologies. My principal question is this: can we actually accomplish this when it comes to truth? In other words, can our ordinary way of employing the vocabulary of truth really be redescribed in such a way as to rid this notion of its "objectivist" implications?

Question 1. Let us begin with the uses of the word true. According to the deflationist position, true is no more than a device of assertion that makes it possible to quote an utterance or disquote it and that, according to the performative conception, also makes it possible to show approval. But there is more to our use of the word true. There are certain highly specific conceptual relations between assertion, belief, and truth, which characterize what I would call the belief-assertion-truth triangle:

a. To affirm something or to make an assertion by means of a statement, is to express one's *belief* that the statement is true (this link is evident in the paradoxical character of statements like "I believe P but P is false," which give rise to what is called Moore's paradox).

b. Truth is the aim or norm of assertion, in the sense that an assertion is correct if and only if it is true (one may of course lie, speak ironically, and so on, but these uses of assertion are derivative with respect to this primary aim and are made possible by it).

c. Truth is also the norm of belief: a belief is correct if and only if it is true. This is often what we mean when we say that beliefs "aim at truth." One can express the same idea by stating that it is a fatal objection against a belief to say that it is false and that a rational subject, if she discovers that one of her beliefs is false, must change it (a subject who admits that she believes a proposition for a reason other than the fact that it is true is irrational in some fashion or else does not have a genuine stance of belief with regard to this proposition).[19]

The deflationist will doubtless reply that (a)—(c) are no more than inoffensive platitudes that do not show in the least that there is anything "normative," in a philosophically important sense, in the notion of truth. He will say to me: "to assert that P is to affirm that P is true and that one believes that P; and to believe that P is to believe that P is true. It is also to believe that one has reasons to believe that P. Of course! But why make such a big deal out of it?" I maintain on the contrary that these conceptual relations are not as trivial as they may seem at first glance. A subject who does not understand that a correct assertion or belief is a true assertion or belief, and that he must satisfy this condition in order to have rational beliefs and utter his assertions correctly, is missing something essential to the notion of truth. By the same token, to describe a community's linguistic use of the word true by saying simply that this word serves to quote and disquote statements the community holds dear is to miss something essential, which is that this word expresses a norm of assertion and belief.[20] This does not mean, as it is sometimes said to do, that the notion of truth is *in itself* normative. For the fact that a statement or a belief is true is a simple fact, a semantic relation existing between the statement or the belief and the world—not a norm. What is normative is the

close connection, roughly described by the conditions a—c, by which truth, belief, and assertion
are mutually bound.

Certain philosophers—with whom I agree—
go farther still in spotlighting this normative ele-
ment proper to the belief-assertion-truth triangle,
by maintaining that the norm of belief and assertion is not simply correct belief but *knowledge*.
Someone who says that P doesn't just represent
herself as believing that P; she is also representing
herself as *knowing* that P, such that her hearers can
ask her "How do you know that?" Now the notion of knowledge, just like that of correct belief,
is a normative notion.[21]

Therefore my first question to Richard Rorty
goes like this: does he think that one can describe
the current practice of assertion, and account for
its link with the ordinary concept of belief, without recourse to the concept of truth and without
recourse to a concept of truth that implies that
there is a norm of our assertions and our beliefs?
In other words, does he intend to deny that the
notion of truth plays a central role in the over-
all system that allows us to express our beliefs
through linguistic communication and to con-

ceive of our beliefs as rational? And, if he thinks that a deflationist theory of truth can account for the normative role of the word true, how does he account for it?

Question 2. I wish to maintain further that the implicit norm of the belief-assertion-truth triangle is equally a norm of *objectivity* for our statements and beliefs. No doubt it is because Rorty admits that the approving and disquotational uses of true are not sufficient to account for what true signifies in our current vocabulary that he accepts the idea that there is a "cautionary" use of the word. But for him, this use signifies no more than the fact that our assertions might be rejected by our hearers. Now, for Rorty, justification is always "relative to an audience." But to that one may object: when someone affirms, in relation to any statement whatsoever, "it is justified, but it isn't true," is she really saying "it is justified for this audience, but not for that audience"? It seems to me, on the contrary, that the contrast is between the reasons we have to believe or justify a statement and the way things are "in reality." Even if one does not believe in an absolute, "external" reality that transcends all our assertions—and it is not necessary to hold this belief in order to use true in this sense—it seems to me that we are indeed establishing a contrast between the reasons for our belief and the facts or reality. Rorty will reply, I imagine, that he does not have this intuition and that he can express it simply as the contrast between justification before one audience and justification before a different audience. But I am unable to grasp how that can be an acceptable description of the sense that *we* give to "true" and not a redescription that leads to a revision, pure and simple, of the sense of this word.[22] If the latter is the case, so be it. But what is there to justify this revision?

Here I suspect that Rorty will reply that my reasoning amounts to a circular argument against the "pragmatist" assimilation of justification to truth: once we have said that a community agrees on a statement, or considers it justified in the sense that it gives its assent to this statement, *the question of knowing whether this statement is true no longer applies* since "warranted assertibility" and "truth" mean the same thing. It is precisely this argument from indistinguishability that leads Rorty to reject the (Peircean) thesis that "truth is the goal of inquiry": when we (we, our community) are in agreement on the fact that snow is white, we may very well say to ourselves "That's true," but saying so does not, in all rigor, add anything more to the content of that on which we are agreed; our agreement suffices, and it is perfectly idle to add that when we acknowledge that snow is white we are aiming at something external to this statement, the true.

An initial response to the argument from indistinguishability might be that it is false to say that the words *true* and *justified* (or *warrantedly assertible*) mean the same thing. If that were the case, the negation of a statement would be the same thing as the affirmation that it is not warrantedly assertible. But to say that the Loch Ness monster does not exist is not the same thing as saying that it is not warrantedly assertible that the Loch Ness monster does not exist.[23] Next, I concede that there is a close link between justification and truth, but this link is not that of identity. When one has reasons, guarantees, or justifications for believing that P, these are justifications for believing that P *is true*. But this does not entail that saying "I am justified in believing that P" and saying "P is true" signify the same thing. On the contrary, this shows that, when one has reasons to assert or believe a proposition, one has reasons to believe that it is *true*. One cannot therefore maintain that *true* and *justified* convey the same thing, since "justified" *presupposes* the very notion of truth. In other words, it seems to me that, despite what Rorty maintains, the disquotational use, the endorsing use, and the cautionary use are not equivalent. Third, and last, let us suppose that we are the victims of a collective brainwashing. Would we want to say in that case that our beliefs were justified in relation to one audience but not in relation to another? No. It seems to me that we would say that our beliefs are justified but false.[24]

Question 3. For the reasons I have indicated above, I am prepared to maintain that the role played by the concept of truth in the belief-assertion-truth triangle, as well as the fact that this concept habitually expresses the possibility of a contrast between our notions and (what I see nothing improper in calling) objective reality, make the concept of truth into a *normative* concept. I am prepared to speak of a norm of truth *in this sense* and am fully aware that this vocabulary runs the very risk to which Rorty continually points: giv-ing the impression that there is a sort of obligation or duty to look for the truth, that it is an intrinsic value or goal of inquiry. But saying that there is a norm of truth for everyday speech does not sig-nify that we must always state the truth or that it is the supreme goal of our inquiries. There is, in other words, no obligation to say or to believe that which is true. I am perfectly ready to agree with Rorty that *the ordinary concept* of truth has nothing "normative" about it in the proto-ethical sense of normative that he decries. What I want to say is simply that truth is a norm of assertion (and of belief) in the sense in which, for any belief what-soever, it is an objection against this belief to say that it is false and that it is *normal* (in the sense that it is the rule) to try to revise it. It is, if you like, a conceptual norm and not an ethical or epistemic norm. This does not mean that it is a psychologi-cal necessity: self-deception and wishful thinking are possible, but we must recognize that these are abnormal behaviors. I am unable to account for these features within a Rortyan framework, that is, within a framework in which the assertion that P is approval that P and in which to believe that

P might aim not at truth but at utility, at what is practical, interesting, or conversationally relevant. So my question is: if one strips the word norm of its "moral" sense while retaining the sense of "rule constitutive of a practice," is Rorty prepared to admit the idea that the true might be the norm of our discursive practices, as much in daily life as in the sciences?

In fact, I often have the impression when reading Rorty that he is developing an argument of the following kind in *modus tollens* (this corresponds to point 5 in my list above):

A if there is a truth as norm or goal of inquiry, then there must be a real property in it such as "the truth of our assertions."

B there is no real property of this kind.

C thus there is no truth as norm or goal of inquiry.

But it seems to me that premise A is false, not, as Rorty all too frequently suggests, because one believes in truth as correspondence or representation in the realist sense but because the fact that there does not exist a property such as the correspondence between our utterance and reality does not entail, *from the point of view of inquiry*, that we are not seeking to attain a certain objective. The notion of a norm does not presuppose the existence of the property in question or its reality. Of course, the discovery that this objective is unattainable or hollow may make us lose all desire to strive for it. But in the relatively innocent sense in which we say that our beliefs aim at truth because it forms part of the concept of belief that if we discover that one of our beliefs is false we try to change it, it seems to me that there is nothing in the least problematic in saying that truth is a norm of belief (and of knowledge).[25]

Question 4. My reason for putting the previous question is that I often have the impression that what Rorty is attacking is a species of transcendental argument which supposedly concludes that, because truth has this normative or conceptual role in our ordinary system of concepts, truth *is* a norm in the more "profound" sense of the goal of inquiry or Supreme Value. But I readily concur with him that there is no argument of this kind. From the fact that truth normatively regulates assertion it does not at all follow that there exist values such as trust, truthfulness, sincerity, or the sense of exactness which are supposed to characterize those who respect the truth. In sum, there is no necessary link between the concept of truth and the concepts of truthfulness or sincerity. It is one thing to say what truth is, to specify the manner in which it functions in our system of belief and assertion, and it is another to say what attitude we ought to adopt in relation to it, or to say what value it ought to have, good or bad. Williams puts the matter well: "The internal role of truth in the belief-assertion-communication system gets us *no further at all* in delivering the values of truthfulness.[26] It is just this type of confusion that veriphobes introduce when they attack the ordinary idea of truth; in the thesis that truth is a norm of assertion they see a form of moralism. This, once again, is the confusion generated by Foucault when he spoke of "the will to truth," and studied social mechanisms like avowal and confession by which truth was valorized. These mechanisms, Foucault proclaims, belong to "the history of truth" and reveal something about the notion of truth, i.e., how it is the product of a certain history, that of the subjectivation and then the objectivation of the concept of truth.[27] But in fact these mechanisms reveal nothing at all about

24

the notion of truth. Foucault and his followers confuse truth with the concept of truth, or with what is believed about truth, and they also confuse truth with the manner in which it is valorized. As soon as one escapes from the grip of this confusion, one perceives the full extent of the difference between the normative conditions for using the concept of truth—which in my view are unchanging[28]—and its use by human individuals or groups, which vary socially and historically. Then the analysis may begin of what Williams calls the "virtues of truth," like sincerity and exactness, and the practices that sustain them (or that flout them, like secrecy and lying). We may also envisage defending these virtues for themselves. There is, of course, a close link between the belief-assertion-truth triangle and the possibility, for example, of lying, since lying could not occur if the triangle did not exist. But that does not mean that the practice of lying, or the practice of sincerity, are entailed by the conceptual triangle in question.

It is therefore necessary to make a sharp distinction between the *conceptual* thesis, according to which truth is a constitutive norm within the belief-assertion–truth triangle, and the *ethical* thesis, according to which it is an intrinsic value and must be respected and sought under all circumstances; and between these two and the *epistemological* thesis according to which it is the goal of inquiry, the supreme epistemic value. One may perfectly well accept the first thesis without accepting the other two. Nevertheless, it ought to be equally clear that there is indeed a link between the norm of truth, the ordinary concept of truth, and the question of our attitudes, ethical or otherwise, concerning truth. When one understands the belief-assertion-truth conceptual linkage, and when one reflects critically on what the fact of having rational beliefs and of revising them in light of available data signifies, it seems very difficult not to admit that truth is *also* a value and that there are certain virtues of truth. By this I do not mean that the conceptual role of truth necessarily entails or justifies ethical principles like "one should not lie" or epistemic principles like "one should only believe a proposition if it is true." Truth can be one thing and the desire for truth can be another. But whoever understands the conceptual role of truth cannot fail to understand how bizarre it is, for example, to believe a proposition despite the fact that one recognises it as being false or because one wishes it were true. Someone might claim, as Rorty generally does, that utility is often more important than truth as a criterion of the value of a concept. But how can one say that a conception is useful if one doesn't know whether it is true? The ostrich may find it useful to plunge its head into the sand. But will that be useful to it "in the long run"?[29] In sum, there is no transcendental deduction of the intrinsic value of the true on the basis of the norm of truth, but the latter is incomprehensible if one fails to grasp what is at stake in the former. On that basis my fourth question for Richard Rorty is this:

Let us assume, like him and contrary to what I have just maintained, that there is only a contingent connection—or even no connection at all—between the conceptual role of truth and the virtues of truth (veracity, sincerity, exactness, trust). Assuming that, how do we analyze these virtues? Are they, as Rorty seems to think, purely instrumental (they are useful) and fully exposed to competition from other virtues such as creativity, interest, and relevance? What conception will a pragmatist in Rorty's sense have of these virtues?

Will he consider, like Nietzsche in *The Geneal-ogy of Morals*, that they are the values of priests or clerics, of men afflicted with *ressentiment*?[30] That they are not virtues at all? That they have little importance and ought to be replaced by other virtues, like Emerson's self-reliance? In particu-lar, does he consider that these virtues are not ones that democracy ought to encourage[31] (this question pertains to point 7 in the list of the-ses above)? Would we even have the nonalethic virtues of solidarity and social utility that Rorty recommends in place of the alethic virtues if the alethic virtues did not exist?

Question 5. This leads me finally to another question, which sums up my reservations about the strategy of replacing vocabularies and about the liberation to which Rortyan pragmatism is supposed to lead us by detaching us from obses-sive worry about the truth.

Should we succeed, both as philosophers and as ordinary individuals and citizens (a distinction Rorty would dislike!), in overcoming our fascina-tion with a language of truth, sincerity, and exact-ness, along with our practical commitment to the values and virtues of truth; in adopting a differ-

ent language and other commitments more in line
with what pragmatism intends; and in conceding
that the notions of truth, sincerity, and so on have
merely instrumental value, that they are means to
other ends (such as democracy, conversation, solidarity, the improvement of our social intercourse
and our life as a community)—what is there to
say that the values and virtues of truth would still
survive in our midst? In other words, if everyone
came to the conclusion that truth is not an intrinsic value to be sought for its own sake and that
its value is only instrumental, would truth survive
even as a mere means to other ends? In my opinion, it would vanish altogther. I have already said
that I do not believe Rorty is an eliminativist pure
and simple with respect to truth and the values of
truth and that I think he wishes above all to rela-
tivize them, to shake off the myths that cling to
them. But would the notion of truth still exist if we
succeeded in abandoning the distinction between
truth and justification? And if we did succeed in
abandoning these ideals and embracing solidarity,
how would that be possible in the absence of individual and collective engagements like trust and
sincerity, which certainly seem to presuppose the

notion of truth? This leads me back to the point with which I began. Why is it that citizens desire trust and sincerity while at the same time they mistrust appeals to sublime and ideal forms of Truth? My answer, which I think is the same as the answer Rorty would give, is that they object to seeing Truth (with a capital *T*) utilized as a handy way to ignore the need for truth (with a lowercase *t*). To put it another way, they are still prepared to think that truth has its uses, just as a lot of other things (especially falsehood) have their uses too. But is that all it comes down to? And, if so, does it follow that people would just as soon that truth (with a lowercase *t*) disappear and that the surrender of this humble truth is desirable? But if truth has no more than instrumental value, as Rorty maintains, how could the virtues of truth even exist?[32]

In conclusion, and without reverting one more time (enough is enough) to the division between the style of philosophy known as continental vis-à-vis the one called analytic, what is the point of the often creditable and praiseworthy efforts made by Rorty in his dialogue with his contemporaries in the analytic camp if even truth (with a lowercase *t*) is devoid of meaning?

MAIN STATEMENT BY Richard Rorty

As Patrick Savidan has remarked, Pascal Engel's philosophical trajectory has been the inverse of my own. Engel was taught the philosophy of Heidegger and Deleuze in school and has ended up working on Tarski and Ramsey. I began with Ayer and Carnap and I ended up writing on Heidegger and praising Derrida. There was indeed a time when I thought that analytic philosophy was the wave of the future. But now I think that it has run out of gas. Except for the work of a handful of iconoclastic geniuses—I am thinking of Kripke, Davidson, and Brandom—the analytic philosophy of recent decades appears to me rather rebarbative and pointless.

So it is understandable that Engel and I do not see eye to eye.

Engel says that my attitude toward the realism–antirealism debate derives from my conviction that the "notion of truth does not designate any substantial property." But I would not use the expression "designate a substantial property." In my view, all descriptive expressions designate properties. The expression *square circle,* the term *infinite number,* the term *democratic,* the expression *being the moon or George Bush*—all of them designate properties. In order to indicate the property that a term designates, all you have to do is add the suffix *-ité* in French, *-heit* in German, or *-ness* in English. One can say *Wahrheit* or *goodness* or *being-the-moon-or-George-Bush-ness.* This procedure will work for any descriptive expression whatever.

In my opinion it is useless to ask which adjectives have a purely expressive function and which designate a property. It is also useless to ask which properties are substantial. All properties, one might say, have the same ontological status. But I should also prefer to abandon expressions like *ontological status.* Pragmatists do not employ this term.

In his book *Truth* Engel cites a description of pragmatism given by Simon Blackburn, which appears to me entirely correct. Blackburn writes that pragmatism is characterized by the "denial of differences, the celebration of the seamless web of language, the soothing away of distinctions, whether of primary versus secondary qualities, fact versus value, description versus expression, of any other significant kind. What is left is a smooth, undifferentiated view of language." Blackburn goes on to say that this view may easily lead to "minimalism, deflationism, quietism."[33]

This is exactly what I take language to be like. It is indeed a seamless web, which can best be understood if we abandon the traditional distinctions. A conception of language as smooth and homogeneous is just the right one to have, and adopting it does indeed lead to quietism.

Engel says that, if this is the pragmatist conception of language, then a pragmatist is the last thing we should be. I will come back to his arguments for this claim. For the moment, I simply wish to emphasize that, for a quietist like me, there is no discourse, debate, theory, or vocabulary that is devoid of meaning. I try to avoid the expression *devoid of meaning.* Any linguistic expression, even an expression like *ontological status,* has a meaning if you give it one. To give meaning to an expression, all you have to do is use it in a more or less predictable manner—situate it within a network of predictable inferences.

The question that matters to us pragmatists is not whether a vocabulary possesses meaning or not, whether it raises real or unreal problems, but whether the resolution of that debate will have an effect in practice, whether it will be useful. We ask whether the vocabulary shared by the debaters is likely to have practical value. For the fundamental thesis of pragmatism is William James's assertion that if a debate has no *practical* significance, then it has no *philosophical* significance.

So my objection to the "realism versus anti-realism" debate is not that the debaters are deploying sentences that are devoid of meaning, nor that they are using terms that do not designate substantial properties. Rather, it is that the resolution of these debates will have no bearing on practice. I view debates of this sort as examples of sterile scholasticism. I regret that such a large part of English-language philosophy in the twentieth century was devoted to questions of this type.

At the beginning of his book *Truth*, Engel rightly says that "most of the history of twentieth-century analytic philosophy is a sort of battlefield opposing various 'realist' and 'anti-realist' conceptions of truth."[34] But when one contemplates not just the history of analytic philosophy alone but that of philosophy in general, one can discern another sort of battle. This one is between those who think it important to discuss realism versus antirealism and those who do their best to show that it is time to leave such questions behind. I am thinking here of Dewey, Davidson, and Brandom, but also of most of the philosophers in the tradition running from Nietzsche to Heidegger, Sartre, and Derrida. My own preference for this tradition rather than for analytic philosophy arises from my conviction that it is less exposed to the risk of scholasticism.

Engel explains in his book that is it possible to feel "that some of the most sophisticated linguistic and logical analyses produced by present-day analytic philosophers come very close to the post-modernist idea that truth is just a word of approval, or a device of assertion of the claims that we like most, and in no way a genuine property."[35] I imagine that he was thinking especially of Davidson and Brandom. It is important, however, to note that neither Davidson nor Brandom employs the notion of substantial property or relies on the distinction between description and expression. These two philosophers share the "smooth," "undifferentiated," "homogeneous" conception of language described by Blackburn. They both attempt to dissolve traditional distinctions. In my opinion, what links the so-called postmodern philosophers to Davidson and Brandom, as well as to the later Wittgenstein, is a rejection of the idea that some discourses, some parts of the culture, are in closer contact with the world, or fit the world better, than other discourses. If one gives up this idea, then one will view every discourse—literary criticism, history, physics, chemistry, plumbers' talk—as on a par, as far as its relation to reality goes. The same relations between thought, language, and reality obtain in every cultural domain. If one discourse has the capacity to represent the world, then all discourses have that capacity. If one of them "fits" the world, then they all do so equally.

Thus the dispute between Engel and myself does not bear on the question of knowing whether there is something that we call objective knowledge. That we use this term is obvious. What divides us is the question whether we should say that certain areas of inquiry attain such knowledge, whereas others unfortunately cannot. I do not like the metaphor of "representing the world" or the one that consists of saying that certain propositions can be "validated" by the world. Yet such metaphors are harmless if we employ them in a nondiscriminatory manner. Our dispute thus has to do with the fact that we give different answers to the question whether or not we should divide the language up into different parts and assert that some have a representational function that others lack.

In addition, our dispute revolves around a related question: what profit can we derive from a description of a part of the culture that, instead of simply explaining its social utility, or determining the degree of consensus that obtains within it, goes on to consider its relation to reality? For the "postmodern" philosophers and the pragmatists (among whom I number myself) the traditional questions of metaphysics and epistemology can be neglected because they have no social utility. It is not that they are devoid of meaning, nor that they rest on false premises; it is simply that the vocabulary of metaphysics and epistemology is of no practical use.

So far I have simply been trying to rectify the description Engel gave of my position. Let me now attempt to reply to the questions he put to me.

I agree with him that one of the main questions that divide us is this: can our ordinary use of the term *true* really be redescribed in such a way as to rid this notion of its objectivist presuppositions? If asserting that there are such presuppositions entails that discriminations between discourses can be made by reference to their ability to produce correspondence to reality, then I think that we should make no such assertion.

Engel says that he is "unable to grasp how that can be an acceptable description of the sense that *we* give to 'true,' and not a redescription that leads to a revision, pure and simple, of the sense of this word." I have no hesitation in saying that I prefer *revision* to *redescription*. On the other hand, I do not think that using the one term rather than the other makes any great difference.

Consider an analogy. When Kant and other Enlightenment thinkers detached moral obligations from divine commands, they did not think that they were revising our moral concepts but that they were describing them more clearly. They were helping us to clarify our conception of morality. The enemies of the Englightenment attacked this claim, accusing these thinkers of *revising* morality. Well, which is it? Did Kant clarify our moral vocabulary, or did he revise it? My feeling is that it is not worth the trouble to try to answer that question. If we adopt the standpoint suggested by the later Wittgenstein and by Quine, we do not need to determine whether a suggested alteration in our linguistic practice counts as a clarification or a revision. The change Kant suggested has contributed to the evolution of our moral discourse. The only question that we need to ask ourselves is this: was this change socially useful, or was it not?

The argument in favor of the modifications that the pragmatists wish to introduce into philosophers' ways of speaking about truth is that we might thereby put an end to some purely scholastic, and by now quite boring, debates between philosophers. The social utility of such a change is obvious.

The most important point, as Savidan has suggested, concerns the question of our responsibilities. If we do things the pragmatist way, we will no longer think of ourselves as having responsibilities toward nonhuman entities such as *truth* or *reality.* I have often suggested that we regard pragmatism as an attempt to complete the project common to the Renaissance humanists and the Enlightenment. The pragmatists think that it is time to stop believing that we have obligations either to God or to some some God surrogate. The pragmatism of James, like the existentialism of Sartre, is an attempt to convince us to stop inventing such surrogates.

Engel is quite right that I interpret the contrast between the truth and those beliefs that appear justified to us in terms of the contrast between future audiences and present-day audiences. The latter will presumably have at their disposal more data, or alternative explanations, or simply greater intellectual sophistication. This way of looking at the matter chimes with my conviction that our responsibilities are exclusively toward other human beings, not toward "reality."

But Engel then poses this question:

> when someone affirms, in relation to any statement whatsoever, "it is justified, but it isn't true," is she really saying "it is justified for this audience, but not for that audience"? It seems to me, on the contrary, that the contrast is between the reasons we have to believe or justify a statement and the way things are "in reality."

I would maintain that a person who says "that belief is justified, but is perhaps not true" should be taken to be distinguishing not between something human and something nonhuman but rather between two situations in which human beings may find themselves: the present situation, in which the belief appears to be justified, and a hypothetical situation in the future, where it will no longer appear justified. I do not claim that this distinction is an accurate analysis of the concepts of justification and truth as they are currently employed. I just want to suggest a way to think about these notions that may have certain advantages. But I have no demonstrable thesis to offer. I am offering either a clarification or a revision and (as I said earlier) I do not care which it is called. Engel, by contrast, is suggesting that we revert to the classical philosophical tradition, which contrasts human consensus with the way nonhuman reality is in itself.

Where does that leave the question of the relation between the concept of truth and the moral virtues mentioned by Engel: truthfulness, sincerity, exactness, and trust? I believe that it is just as easy to inculcate these virtues by reference to our practices of justification as by insisting on the importance of truth. A person is sincere when she says what she thinks she is justified in believing. This will, automatically, be what she believes to be true. So I think that we could promote the relevant virtues without ever needing to contrast truth with mere justification. On the other hand, I do not believe, contrary to what Engel suggests, that warranted assertibility and truth are the same thing. In certain contexts the two are interchangeable, but in others they are not. One cannot, for example, use *warranted assertibility* to describe the property preserved in valid inference. But when it comes to inculcating habits of exactness, or creat-

ing a climate of trust, it matters little which notion one deploys.

I do not believe that people will become less
sincere or less concerned to be precise because
they have become pragmatists. More generally, I
do not think that the fact of speaking as I do,
rather than according to the guidelines recom-
mended by Engel, would make any difference in
the ways people behave when they are not engag-
ing in philosophical discussions. When the thinkers of the Enlightenment dissociated moral delib-
eration from divine commands, their writings did
not provoke any notable increase in the amount
of immorality. So I do not see why the separation
of the notion of "truth" from that of "reality in
itself" should produce either increased insincerity
or a willingness to be deluded.

And so to the last question: is truth a normative concept? I am not sure I understand Engel's
use of *normative concept*. If he simply means that
we should try to have only true beliefs, then we
do not disagree. If, on the other hand, he means
that truth is an intrinsic good, that it possesses an
intrinsic value, then the question seems to be un-
discussable. I do not have the faintest idea how to

go about determining which goods are the intrinsic ones and which are the instrumental ones. Nor do I see the point of raising the question. *Intrinsic* is a word that pragmatists find it easy to do without. If one thinks that sincerity and exactness are good things, I do not see why we should worry about whether they are means to something else or good in themselves. Which reply one gives to such questions will have no bearing on practice. Trying never to have anything but true beliefs will not lead us to do anything differently than if we simply try our best to justify our beliefs to ourselves and to others.

Consider, in this connection, the analogy between beliefs and actions. James notoriously said that "the true" is what is "good in the way of belief."[36] Trying to do the right thing will lead us to do just the same things we would do when we try to justify our actions to ourselves and others. We do not have any way to establish the truth of a belief or the rightness of an action except by reference to the justifications we offer for thinking what we think or doing what we do. The philosophical distinction between justification and truth seems not to have practical consequences. That is why pragmatists think it is not worth pondering.

In conclusion, I would remark that since Plato the meanings of normative terms like *good, just* and *true* have been problems only for philosophers. Everybody else knows how to use them and does not need an explanation of what they mean. I am perfectly ready to admit that one cannot identify the concept of truth with the concept of justification or with any other. But that is not a sufficient reason to conclude that the nature of truth is an important or interesting question.

Discussion

Pascal Engel

No doubt I may have portrayed Richard Rorty's positions inadequately in some respects, and I regard the clarifications he has proposed as highly constructive. Nonetheless, I do wish to return to certain difficulties, but with a slight shift of perspective, so as not to simply reiterate the points of disagreement.

I am a little surprised that Rorty endorses the characterization of pragmatism that I had quoted from Simon Blackburn, who depicts this school as having a "seamless" conception of reality and language. As far as I know, we normally regard the task of philosophy as that of detecting, even producing, differences. One thinks of the famous words in *King Lear*, "I'll teach you differences," to which Wittgenstein refers in criticizing Hegel.[37] I have the feeling that, for Rorty's part, he is saying, "I'll teach you sameness." What he claims is "I am going to show you the similitude, the identity, between things."

The debates to which Rorty alludes, the one on realism-antirealism for example, are admittedly technical matters, to which philosophers have dedicated a great deal of effort, and in certain cases the law of diminishing returns does indeed apply: some of these debates have turned into sterile exercises in scholasticism. Still, I find that the remedy Rorty proposes is worse than the disease. His proposal to ignore distinctions like the ones between *instrumental* and *intrinsic* or between *expression* and *description* also has significant drawbacks.

No doubt Rorty will not agree with me on this point, but it does seem to me that some of the debates about whether certain types of statement or affirmation really have truth value are important ones, if we wish to grasp the distinctions that have to be made between the different modes of discourse. Let us leave science aside and take the case of moral discourse. There is a conception called expressivism, which defends the view that, when I say "torture is evil," all I am doing is expressing my mental (or other) state. The opposing conception consists in the affirmation that this is a properly formed statement expressing a belief that may be true or false. Rorty regards this problem as pointless, if I follow him correctly. He takes the view that, whatever answer we give, it would make no difference to our practice. I obviously feel, on the contrary, that it is extremely important in this domain and in others to be able to grasp differences.

What Rorty is proposing is really revolutionary. In fact, a good part of what literary criticism and the philosophy of science do is to ask whether there are different degrees of objectivity to discourses. If we say that all discourses are equally valid, then a certain number of philosophers will indeed be out of a job. But that is not really the heart of the problem. To state that there is no difference between discourses entails consequences that we may regard as detrimental. For instance, Rorty often says that science is "a kind of writing," and he does not see much difference between philosophical writing and literature. I may be old-fashioned, but I do see differences. And I do see the dangers of teaching Spinoza and Russell in literature departments or Proust in philosophy departments. In this connection I have a question I would like to put to Rorty, which seems to me really very important for his thought: I am talking about the question of redescription. Rorty has offered us a rather deflationist version of this notion of redescription, indicating that the important thing about it is the nature of the change it would introduce into practices.

This raises two problems from my perspective. First, is Rorty himself not committing the mistake of which he accuses his adversaries? In other words, doesn't he make too much of the opposition between a representationist, realist conception of truth, on one hand, and a pragmatist conception of it, like his own, on the other? Do persons who use the word *true,* who speak of *objectivity,* who distinguish between *justification* and *truth,* subscribe to a correspondentist theory of truth by doing so? Do they need to subscribe to the truth-making idea? I do not think so. I am ready to defend the view that some sort of distinction is necessary, but the fact that we make use of it does not mean that we are relapsing into the errors of Platonism. So I perceive a certain form of hypostasis in Rorty's way of proceeding.

Let me now turn to the second difficulty to which Rorty's concept of redescription seems to me to give rise. There are certainly many re-descriptions that turn out to be inoffensive and insignificant. For example, the students who occupied the Sorbonne in 1968 tended to call what they were doing a *revolution*. Quite soon after, this *revolution* came to be called an *event*. Here we are dealing with a relatively correct redescription. But a redescription can have quite serious consequences from the point of view of values. When Jean-Marie Le Pen calls the Shoah a *detail*, that too is a redescription. But it seems to me a redescription of a quite different kind from the pre-ceeding one. So my question is this: does Rorty think the fact that there is a change of vocabulary will have no effect on the values in question? I see no objection to getting rid of the word *true*. We could perfectly well decide to replace it with the word *frue*.[38] Thus I would refer to a statement of what I took to be the case as *frue* rather than as *true*. But that is not the problem, as Rorty will agree. The problem is not the description as such but the kinds of impact certain redescriptions may have on values.

For that matter, as regards the kind of debate that Rorty invites us to set aside as being scholastic and without practical consequences, I am inclined to think that his argument depends a great deal on what one understands by "practical consequences." With respect to almost any kind of pure theorising, there are no practical consequences. But certain debates do have consequences on certain styles of theorizing. The opposition between realism and antirealism does play a role in certain areas, even within the development of knowledge. In mathematics, for example, the opposition between intuitionism and Platonism is an extremely lively debate. Does Rorty really think that this debate is entirely hollow?

With regard to the scholastic character, or not, of these debates, it becomes extremely difficult to assess that as soon as we start to look at practical consequences. This objection was already being raised in the time of William James. In the field of ethics, for example, there are numerous debates on questions of bioethics, applied ethics, and so on. When I read works of this kind, I confess that I quite often find them boring and scholastic; they introduce all kinds of quite useless distinctions or they ignore absolutely fundamental distinctions that have been marked out in the domain of metaethics. I often find them tiresome and theoretically stunted. And yet, paradoxically, as soon as you start doing applied ethics, it is understood that others may possibly draw practical consequences from what you have to say. So should we do away with departments of logic and metaphysics, of the kind that exist in Scotland, and replace them with departments of applied ethics? If that is Rorty's prescription, I find it a little dangerous.

Richard Rorty

I think that Engel is right: on one hand, I defend a deflationist conception of redescription, but, on the other, I suggest that redescribing things in my way is not very important. I think that redescription is an important task, carried out not by philosophers but by all sorts of intellectuals. They change the way we use words, and by doing so they build new intellectual worlds. This has been going on ever since Plato and Socrates. Descartes, for example, transformed and partially replaced the vocabulary of scholasticism. He thereby helped bring a new way of doing philosophy into being. Another example is the way in which the thinkers of the Enlightenment transformed moral discourse. It is not my intention to say that a redescription is without importance. But I do want to insist that what analytic philosophers call conceptual clarification or conceptual analysis is never anything more than disguised redescription. Analytic philosophers often compliment themselves on being "more scientific" than other philosophers, but they are doing no more than what intellectuals have always done: suggesting new ways of speaking, proposing linguistic practices that are different from those that currently prevail.

The positivists who, having adopted a noncognitivist theory of ethics, claimed that the assertion "torture is an evil" was neither true nor false, were suggesting that we needed to change our linguistic habits. But this redescription was not an invitation to engage in torture. Positivism is grounded, in general, in the notion that there is something important that can be called "the search for truth" and that the paradigm of this search is empirical science, the area of culture that supposedly is in closest contact with reality. The positivists proposed various redescriptions that would make the paradigmatic status of empirical inquiry more evident.

The tendency to promote certain areas of culture to a position of dominance is entirely natural. I simply want to emphasize that, when considering the hierarchies proposed by those making such attempts, we should not think of them as anything more than parts of a particular cultural-political initiative. We ought not to imagine that philosophers possess a particular technique allowing them, for example, to discover whether the sentence "torture is an evil" can be either true or false. Philosophers have pretended that the question whether it can be—whether moral judgments are candidates for the status of objective knowledge—is a profound and important one. My own feeling is that the question was raised only in order to suggest that certain areas of culture should be privileged over others.

Engel has adduced the distinction between intuitionism and Platonism in mathematics, asking me whether I think that this distinction is "hollow." Some mathematicians take this topic seriously, while others regard it as a problem for philosophers of mathematics and not for "real" mathematicians—the latter being the people who do not give the question a second thought. I do not know which mathematicians are right. But I suspect that if we were to consign the question of the ontological status of mathematical entities to oblivion, the progress of mathematics would not be affected.

Pascal Engel

Does Rorty not agree, first of all, that the philosophers who have counted for him, like Quine and Davidson, have discussed these problems of ontological status at length? And that consequently the debt he owes to their work, and thus to work of this *type*, is not negligible? One might also wonder whether they have definitively resolved these questions. I have my doubts. Next, the distinction he makes between questions that have practical incidence and purely empty and scholastic questions reminds me of the contrast the positivist Rudolf Carnap used to posit between "internal" questions and "external" questions. For Rorty, obviously, questions about the ontology of mathematics are typically "external" questions. He said at the start that he makes no distinction between that which is devoid of meaning and that which is not. I wonder whether the fact of distinguishing between that which has practical consequences and that which does not have them doesn't amount in a way to reintroducing a criterion of the meaningfulness of concepts. Perhaps, in the end, Rorty is just as much a positivist as King Carnap.

Richard Rorty

As regards Carnap, I would simply say that his distinction between what is internal and what is external to a system presupposes a distinction between analytic and synthetic truths. But after Quine there was not much left of the latter distinction. So the distinction proposed by Carnap was no longer of much use. We do not have any clear way to locate the boundary between the internal and the external.

We can employ the contrast between questions that are worth tackling and those that make no difference without ever utilizing notions like *meaning* or *sense*. There is no need to insult people who are engaged in discussing traditional philosophical distinctions by declaring that their reflections are empty of meaning or that the expressions they use are devoid of sense. We can dispense with such positivist insults and ask simply: "Why go to so much trouble?" Engel is right to point out that Quine devoted much thought to the opposition between Platonism and intuitionism. But many other philosophers, such as Davidson and Brandom, see no reason to do so. On this point, I think they are wiser than Quine. Brandom adheres to the conception of language we saw characterized by Blackburn. His great merit lies in the fact that he doesn't bother trying to recapture the traditional distinctions. You will find plenty of distinctions in his work, but they are not the ones that philosophers have traditionally discussed.

Finally I am tempted to say that we have given many of these traditional distinctions their chance. We have debated them ad infinitum, without that having had any practical upshot. So I propose that from now on we focus on other distinctions.

Pascal Engel: *Truth*

Richard Rorty

Pascal Engel, who teaches at the Sorbonne, is one of the leading figures in the ongoing attempt to make the disciplinary matrix of French philosophy more like that of Anglo-American philosophy and to get French philosophers to take seriously the problems discussed by their Anglophone colleagues. In this book he offers a clear, succinct, and very useful review of discussions of

Review by Richard Rorty of Pascal Engel, *Truth* (Montreal: McGill-Queen's University Press, 2002; published in Britain by Acumen Press). *Notre Dame Philosophical Reviews,* 2003: http://ndpr.nd.edu/.

the concept of truth by such figures as Moore, Ramsey, Strawson, Davidson, Wright, Rorty, Horwich, and Putnam.

Engel thinks it important to acknowledge the advantages of deflationist views—views that take truth as a primitive and unanalyzable notion—but equally important to block the road from deflationism to positions (such as Foucault's, Latour's, and Rorty's) that smack of "nihilism," "skepticism," and "relativism." So he formulates and defends a compromise position that he calls "minimal realism."

Engel agrees with Wright, "if we described the practice of a community who had a device of assertion without mentioning that assertions aim at truth, or if we described people as having beliefs without these aiming at truth, our description would be incomplete and inadequate" (92).

But he differs from Wright in insisting, "the norm of truth is the norm of *realist*, recognition-transcendent truth" (93). For "a minimalism about *truth* does not imply a minimalism about truth-*aptness.*" In each domain of inquiry, "truth-aptness is to be judged after the realist criterion of the independence of a domain from our responses"

(89). So we have to "reconcile our epistemology of the concepts involved in each domain with the account of the truth of propositions involving them" (123).

Engel says, "deflationism about truth pays a lot of dividends, but it has to pay the price" (56). One such price is being unable to account for "the fact that truth is the point of assertion." He cites Dummett as saying that omitting the fact that assertion and belief aim at truth is "like omitting the fact that the purpose of playing a game is to win it" (58). Another price is leaving us unable to compare the status of truths in one domain (say science) to that of truth in another domain (say ethics or fiction). Still another is an inability to handle the distinction between metaphorical and literal truth. "If some sentences fail to be literally true or to be apt for truth, the deflationist should give us an account of this" (59).

Engel grants that some deflationists, such as Rorty, are willing to "bite the bullet," claiming that it is a virtue of their view that it sweeps aside these and other traditional distinctions, thereby dissolving many traditional philosophical problems. But he rightly points out, "the sophisticated attempts of analytic philosophers at constructing minimalist theories of truth" do not "automatically lead to the kind of nihilism and skepticism illustrated by Rorty." "There is," he rightly says, "a theoretical ambition in the former that is absent from the latter" (63).

Engel has two sorts of arguments against deflationism. The first consists in pointing out that deflationists cannot accept certain familiar platitudes, such as that inquiry converges to truth or that true sentences have a relation called "correspondence" to their subjects that false sentences do not. The other sort is metaphilosophical: "The reason why you need to have a robust conception of truth condition is ... that minimalism about truth-aptness robs all sorts of debates of any sense" (119).

If those debates are held to be pointless, any "theoretical ambition" one might have had in this area of inquiry will quickly drain away.

The first set of arguments relies on the reader agreeing that it would be absurd to abandon a certain intuition. The second relies on her agreeing that it would be absurd to claim that a certain long-lasting philosophical debate should never have been begun. Neither can be conclusive, since a hardened bullet biter will always try to make a virtue of necessity. He will urge that letting go of certain intuitions, or letting certain debates lapse, is the price of intellectual progress. Arguments about what does and does not constitute such progress are about as inconclusive as philosophical arguments can get.

This inconclusiveness is best illustrated by reflection on the upshot of the metaphilosophical portions of Engel's book, particularly chapter 4, "The Realist/Anti-realist Controversies." Here Engel points out how many of the controversies between analytic philosophers presuppose that some parts of culture are more truth-apt than others. The blithe indifferentism of Arthur Fine's "NOA" (the Natural Ontological Attitude, which many deflationists adopt) "threatens to undercut all epistemological questions about scientific theories" (105). Again, "if there is no way of distinguishing description of matters of fact from expression of attitudes, any sort of meta-ethical view, be it realist or anti-realist, is absurd" (109).

Engel's French colleagues who doubt that contemporary Anglophone philosophy is a model worthy of imitation can accept everything Engel says about the need for a notion of truth-aptness if we are to keep epistemology and metaethics going. But they will then reverse the argument. Since those subdisciplines have degenerated into terminal dreariness, they will say, it would be a good idea to get rid of truth-aptness, thereby hastening their demise. Skeptics of this sort can happily agree with Engel that "most of the history of twentieth-century analytic philosophy is a sort of battlefield opposing various 'realist' and 'anti-realist' conceptions of truth" (4). But they think that the battlefield has been trampled into a quagmire.

Notes

INTRODUCTION

1. Unpublished manuscript: http://www.stanford.edu/~rrorty/pragmatistview.htm.

2. Richard Rorty, *Philosophy and the Mirror of Nature* (Princeton: Princeton University Press, 1979).

3. Unpublished manuscript: http://www.stanford.edu/~rrorty/pragmatistview.htm.

4. Ibid.

WHAT'S THE USE OF TRUTH?

1. Williams makes this observation, with which I agree, in *Truth and Truthfulness*, p. 1. Rorty's review

of Williams's book appeared in the *London Review of Books* for October 31, 2002.

2. The English words *true* and *trust* have the same etymology, which makes the contrast more piquant in this language.

3. See Goldman, *Knowledge in a Social World*, pp. 5–7 and p. 370, where he draws a contrast between *veriphobia* and *veritism*.

4. Cf. Alan D. Sokal and Jean Bricmont, *Fashionable Nonsense. Postmodern Philosophers' Abuse of Science* (New York: Picador, 1998); and Alan D. Sokal, *The Sokal Hoax. The Sham that Shook the Academy* (Lincoln: University of Nebraska Press, 2000). For my part I preferred to deal with the affair ironically; cf. Pascal Engel, "L'affaire Sokal concerne-t-elle les philosophes français?" in J.-F. Mattei, *Philosopher en français* (Paris: PUF, 2000).

5. "Solatium miseris socios habuisse malorum," Jacques Bouveresse, Alan Sokal, and Jean Bricmont. Two examples of accusations of this kind addressed to the present author specifically are C. Chauviré, "Faut-il moraliser les normes cognitives?" and Sandra Laugier, "Pourquoi des théories morales?" in *Cités* 5 (2001), and my reply, cowritten with Kevin Mulligan, "Normes éthiques et normes cognitives."

6. In saying this, I am bound to give the impression of believing that it is GOOD to be an analytic philosopher and BAD not to be one and so of committing the type of *petitio principii* of which Rorty has often accused me; cf. his text in response to Jacques Bouveresse in Cometti, *Lire Rorty*, pp. 154–155, in which he takes to task my article "The Analytic-Continental Divide." Readers may rest assured: I think that being an analytic philosopher provides no immunity against bad philosophy. But that is not what matters here. What does matter is that Rorty is someone who is capable of understanding a number of different philosophical vocabularies and finding the common ground between them. In this he is highly unusual, as Jacques Bouveresse remarks in *Lire Rorty*, p. 25.

7. He is open to the imputation of systematically reading these authors in ways that suit his own purposes. I have stated my reservations about Rorty's manner of reading Davidson in *Davidson et la philosophie du langage*, pp. 262–264.

8. For an analysis of the differences, cf. C. Tiercelin, "Un pragmatisme conséquent?"

9. On these positions, see especially Rorty's "Pragmatism, Davidson, and Truth."

10. Bertrand Russell's analyses of the pragmatist theory of truth in his *Philosophical Essays* (1910) remain unsurpassed.

11. They are set out in my books *La vérité* and *Truth*. These are distinct works, despite the similarity of the titles.

12. Williams, *Truth and Truthfulness*, pp. 128–129.

13. Rorty has defended this idea forcefully against Crispin Wright in "Is Truth a Goal of Inquiry?"

14. One may compare the debate about the distinction between expressivism and emotivism in ethics. Cf. Gibbard, *Wise Choices, Apt Feelings*; and Blackburn, *Ruling Passions*. If Rorty means to defend an expressivist conception of truth and say that *true* does not denote a real property but is simply an ejaculation, then he runs up against the objections classically raised by Peter Geach (in "Assertion") with regard to the expressivist position: if the premises of an argument are neither true nor false, how can the argument be valid in the classic sense in which the truth of the premises is supposed to be preserved in the conclusion? This raises another, more technical, question, which I would like to put to Rorty: to what extent does he consider that pragmatism, and the assimilation

of truth to warranted assertibility, compel us to modify our logic?

15. This view is often attributed to Ramsey; cf. Ramsey, "Facts and Propositions." For reservations about this reading of Ramsey, see Dokic and Engel, *Ramsey, Truth, and Success.*

16. Especially on the basis of the "slingshot" argument; cf. Engel, *The Norm of Truth*, pp. 26–27; and, in the original French, *La norme du vrai*, p. 18. In his book *Facing Facts*, Neale maintains that although this argument does not succeed in *refuting* theories about facts, it does *constrain* them in an important way. Cf. as well Dodd, *An Identity Theory of Truth.*

17. Cf. Dokic and Engel, *Ramsey, Truth, and Success.*

18. Cf. Engel, "Is Truth a Norm?" and *Truth*, chapter 5.

19. I have analyzed the sense in which to believe is to aim at truth in "Truth and the Aim of Belief," in Gillies, *Laws and Models in Science.*

20. This idea was very clearly advanced by Dummett in "Truth."

21. This is the thesis of Williamson, in particular, in *Knowledge and Its Limits*, although he rejects the classical assimilation of knowledge to justified true belief.

22. See the dialogue between McDowell and Rorty in Brandom, *Rorty and His Critics*, pp. 108–128.

23. The line of reasoning is of the kind given by Wright in *Truth and Objectivity*, chapter 1.

24. In his review of Williams's *Truth and Truthfulness* in the *London Review of Books*, Rorty replies that this argument commits a *petitio principii* against him by taking for granted that there exists a way of comparing our representations to an external reality. To me it seems that the point being made here is simply that the two terms cannot have the same meaning. In his extremely interesting reading of George Orwell's *1984* in *Contingency, Irony, and Solidarity*, Rorty maintains that O'Brien's famous statement "freedom is the freedom to say that $2 + 2 = 4$" does *not* show that Orwell defends an objectivist ideal. There is just one party who engages in brainwashing and another who is the victim of it, but nothing to separate them *objectively*. This is a fascinating reading, but once again I find that Rorty carries things a little too far.

25. Cf. the exchange, in Brandom, *Rorty and His Critics*, between Akeel Bilgrami and Rorty. Bilgrami contrasts the first-person viewpoint of the inquirer to the third-person viewpoint of truth as a real

property, and maintains that the arguments of Rorty (and on this point, of Davidson) do not in the least undermine the description of the first of these viewpoints as aiming at truth.

26. Williams, *Truth and Truthfulness*, p. 85.

27. Foucault, *L'Herménetique du sujet*, pp. 19–31; in English in Foucault, *The Hermeneutics of the Subject*, pp. 14–30.

28. I agree with G.E. Moore when he says that there is no history of truth, although doubtless there is a history of our beliefs regarding truth; see "Truth and Falsity," p. 22. The historicist conception of truth owes a great deal to Detienne's *The Masters of Truth in Archaic Greece*, which, although it is often utilized to justify the confusion between truth and our conceptions of the truth, contains no trace of such confusion.

29. This is an argument of classic pragmatism, that of Ramsey for example: useful beliefs are true in the long run, and they are useful *because* they are true. Cf. Dokic and Engel, *Ramsey, Truth, and Success*.

30. Williams, *Truth and Truthfulness*, chapter 2, makes a laudable, but not totally convincing, effort to propound the view that Nietzsche was really a defender of these virtues.

31. As I have already noted, this is an essential component of Rorty's pragmatism. In his book *Achieving Our Country. Leftist Thought in Twentieth-Century America* (Cambridge: Harvard University Press, 1998), he takes the American left to task for having adopted a purely intellectual and "on-looker" attitude and ceding the values of action to the right. He correctly charges this left with having become sardonic and "Foucauldian." But, even allowing for the fact that objectivist ideals and the virtues of truth are currently preached in the United States by the right, and the administration of George W. Bush, is that a reason for the left to shun them? The events of 2003, among others, show to what extent a defense of the virtues of truth can go hand in hand with the utmost hypocrisy. Does that mean we have to renounce them?

32. This is the question posed by Williams in *Truth and Truthfulness*, p. 59.

33. Engel, *Truth*, p. 141, quoting Blackburn, *Ruling Passions*, p. 157.

34. Ibid., p. 4.

35. Ibid., p. 6.

36. *"The true is the name of whatever proves itself to be good in the way of belief, and good too for defi-*

nite, assignable reasons." William James, *Pragmatism*, lecture 2, "What Pragmatism Means" (1907), in *Pragmatism and Other Writings*, p. 38 (emphasis in the original).

37. This remark by Wittgenstein is reported in Rhees, *Recollections of Wittgenstein*, p. 157.

38. This was the word proposed by Tarski in his classic piece "The Semantic Concept of Truth" (1940), in *Readings in Philosophical Analysis*, p. 66.

Bibliography

Blackburn, Simon. *Ruling Passions*. Oxford: Oxford University Press, 1998.

Brandom, Robert, ed. *Rorty and His Critics*. Oxford: Blackwell, 2000.

Cometti, J.-P., ed. *Lire Rorty*. Combas: L'Éclat, 1992.

Detienne, Marcel. *The Masters of Truth in Archaic Greece*. Trans. Janet Lloyd. New York: Zone, 1996.

Dodd, J. *An Identity Theory of Truth*. London and New York: McMillan–St. Martin's, 2001.

Dokic, Jérôme, and Pascal Engel. *Ramsey, Truth, and Success*. London: Routledge, 2002.

Dummet, Michael. "Truth." *Proceedings of the Aristotelian Society* 59 (1959): 141–162; rpt. in Dummett, *Truth and Other Enigmas*. London: Duckworth, 1978.

Engel, Pascal. *Davidson et la philosophie du langage*. Paris: PUF, 1994.

———— "Is Truth a Norm?" In P. Pagin, P. Kotatko

and G. Segal, eds., *Interpreting Davidson*. Stanford: CSLI, 2000, pp. 37–51.

———— *La norme du vrai*. 3d ed. Paris: Gallimard, 2003 [1989].

———— *La vérité*. Paris: Hatier, 1998.

———— "The Analytic-Continental Divide." *Stanford French Review* 17 (1993).

———— *The Norm of Truth*. Toronto: University of Toronto Press, 1991.

———— *Truth*. Montreal: McGill-Queen's University Press, 2002.

———— "Truth and the Aim of Belief." In Donald Gillies, ed., *Laws and Models in Science,* pp. 79–99. London: King's College, 2004.

———— Review of Charles Guignon and David Hiley, eds., *Richard Rorty*. Cambridge: Cambridge University Press, 2003. *Notre Dame Philosophical Reviews,* 2004: http://ndpr.nd. edu/

Engel, Pascal, and Kevin Mulligan. "Normes éthiques et normes cognitives." In *Cités* 15 (2003): 171–186.

Foucault, Michel. *L'Herménetique du sujet. Cours au Collège de France, 1981–1982*. Ed. Frédéric Gros. Paris: Gallimard–Le Seuil, 2001.

———— *The Hermeneutics of the Subject: Lectures at the Collège de France, 1981–1982*. Ed. Frédéric

Gros, trans. Graham Burchell. London: Palgrave-Macmillan, 2005.

Geach, Peter. "Assertion." *Philosophical Review* 74 (1965): 449–465.

Gibbard, Alan. *Wise Choices, Apt Feelings*. Harvard: Harvard University Press, 1991.

Goldman, Alvin I. *Knowledge in a Social World*. Oxford: Oxford University Press, 1999.

James, William. *Pragmatism and Other Writings*. Ed. Giles Gunn. New York: Penguin, 2000.

Moore, G.E. "Truth and Falsity." In G. E. Moore, *Philosophical Writings*. Ed. T. Baldwin. London: Routledge, 1993.

Neale, Stephen. *Facing Facts*. Oxford: Oxford University Press, 2002.

Ramsey, F. "Facts and Propositions." In *Philosophical Papers*. Cambridge: Cambridge University Press, 1990.

Rhees, Rush. *Recollections of Wittgenstein*. Oxford: Oxford University Press, 1984.

Rorty, Richard. *Achieving Our Country. Leftist Thought in Twentieth-Century America*. Cambridge: Harvard University Press, 1998.

———— *Contingency, Irony, and Solidarity*. Cambridge: Cambridge University Press, 1989.

——— "Is Truth a Goal of Inquiry? Davidson vs. Wright." *Philosophical Quarterly* 45 (1995): 281–300.

——— *Philosophy and the Mirror of Nature.* Princeton: Princeton University Press, 1979.

——— "Pragmatism, Davidson, and Truth." In E. LePore, ed., *Truth and Interpretation.* Oxford: Blackwell, 1985.

——— Review of Williams, *Truth and Truthfulness,* in *London Review of Books,* October 31, 2002.

Tarski, Alfred. "The Semantic Concept of Truth." In H. Feigl and W. Sellars, ed., *Readings in Philosophical Analysis.* Englewood Cliffs, NJ.: Prentice-Hall, 1949.

Tiercelin, C. "Un pragmatisme conséquent?" In C. Chauviré, ed., *Jacques Bouveresse, parcours d'un combattant,* special ed. of *Critique,* nos. 567–568, pp. 642–660. Paris: Minuit, 1994.

Williams, Bernard. *Truth and Truthfulness. An Essay in Genealogy.* Princeton: Princeton University Press, 2002.

Williamson, T. *Knowledge and Its Limits.* Oxford: Oxford University Press, 2000.

Wright, Crispin. *Truth and Objectivity.* Oxford: Oxford University Press, 1992.